HONUA

HONUA

Sage U'ilani Takehiro

Kahuaomānoa Press
Honolulu, Hawai'i
a collaboration with Kuleana 'Ōiwi Press

~Kahuaomānoa Press~

President & Chief Editor	Brandy Nālani McDougall
Vice-President & Managing Editor	Ann Inoshita
Associate Editor & Treasurer	Ryan Oishi
Assistant Editors	Kai Gaspar, Emelihter Kihleng
Hawaiian Language Editor	Bryan Kamaoli Kuwada
Corresponding Editor	ku'ualoha ho'omanawanui
Typesetting & Book Design	Brent Fujinaka
Cover Design	Kūha'o Zane, Ethnic Creative
	(kuhao@ethniccreative.com)

Kahuaomānoa means, in 'ōlelo Hawai'i, "the fruit of Mānoa"
and "foundation of Mānoa."

Kahuaomānoa Press is dedicated toward the publication and promotion
of excellence in student art and literature. As such, every effort is made
to privilege the student voice and perspective first and foremost.

The poems "Vacation on Hawai'i's Big Island" and "Ka Wai Lani o Hilo"
are anthologized in *'Ōiwi: A Native Hawaiian Journal 3.*

Shout Outs

Kalawaianui. Takehiro mochi. Chao clan. Lau-lau. Lau-ye. Tutu Lady. Tutu Man. Momma. Daddy. Roobs. Jace. Graces. Aokis. Uncles. Aunties. Cuzins. Hilo. BI. Underground. Halau O Kekuhi. Halau Ku Mana. This is to the Girls in the High Heel Shoes, love baby love. They mamas and papas. Da boys/bitches. JFS. No Regrets. PMG. 789. Imua Kamehameha. Robert the poet Sullivan. Susan the slugger Schultz. Morgan no no no that's crap Blair. Ruth wine is good Hsu. JC of Honors '05 and Leimomi. Candace Fujikane. Cynthia Franklin. Noenoe Silva. David Sing. Kuualoha Hoomanawanui. UHM Eng Dept and the "colleagues" hehehe, wha wha whuuut! Kuy 402. CRDG. Puna CC. Ethnic Creative. The Cut. Fearless Hawaiians. 808 Empire. The Fruit of Manoa. Bran and da crew. You know how we do. To those I've ever hurt, I am truly sorry. To those who have hurt me, you suck, but thanks anyway, I still your friend. To my 'ohana, I would die for you, but good thing I stay living for you instead. To the owls, thanks for making sure I get home safely after all those late nights. To the sharks thanks for making sure I don't drown. To the man with the master plan, Jesus loves me. Aloha ke Akua a me na 'aumakua. Mahalo piha. Peace.

Contents

Foreword

Our bones hide from bulldozers
in the dirt breast of our mother
while the bones of our ancestors
breathe under our brown skin
born from the same darkness
As the Moʻo
We change colors—
Mana Never Dies.
                    ~E Hui Pū~

Honua: 1. nvs. Land, earth, world; background, as of quilt design; basic, at
the foundation, fundamental. (*Hawaiian Dictionary*).

In many ways, *Honua* is a first, laying a new foundation: the first col-
lection of poetry by Kanaka Maoli (Native Hawaiian) writer Sage
Uʻilani Takehiro. The first publication in a new series of student writ-
ing coming out of UH Mānoa called Kahuaomānoa. The first collabo-
ration between Kahuaomānoa and Kuleana ʻŌiwi Press, a non-profit
organization dedicated to promoting Kanaka Maoli literature and arts,
and our primary publication, *ʻŌiwi: A Native Hawaiian Journal.*

For thousands of years, Kanaka Maoli were excellent haku mele,
composers of chants, hula, and songs which celebrated our love for our
ʻāina (land), culture, heritage, and traditions; haʻi moʻolelo, storytellers
who recounted the great deeds of our gods, ancestors, and heroes; ipu
moʻokūʻauhau, keepers of the genealogies who remembered the great
deeds of our beloved chiefs, reminding us of the familial connection
between kanaka (people), lani (sky) and honua (earth).

When western literacy—reading and writing—were introduced to
Hawaiʻi in the early 19th century, Kanaka Maoli began writing prolif-
ically, recording everything they could on paper. When print technol-
ogy normalized the distribution of newspapers, by mid-century, a
number of Kanaka Maoli-run nūpepa (newspapers) continued the long
line of oral tradition from haku mele, haʻi moʻolelo, and ipu
moʻokūʻauhau with a new media, ka palapala (literature). Aside from
writing down traditional orature, such as oli, mele, hula, kanikau
(laments), and moʻolelo, under the influence of outside, primarily
western culture, literature from distant lands, such as *Arabian Nights*,
Brothers Grimm fairy tales, and *20,000 Leagues Under the Sea,* were
published alongside traditional and newly composed Kanaka Maoli
stories. Kanaka Maoli wrote prolifically throughout the nineteenth and

early twentieth century, producing over one million manuscript pages of printed text in the span of about one hundred years, with countless more written manuscripts and mele books existing today in public and private collections.

The slow disenfranchisement and silencing of Kanaka Maoli from the political arena which began in the mid-19th century ultimately resulted in the overthrow of the Hawaiian government in 1893 and the closing of schools of ʻōlelo Hawaiʻi by 1896, and annexation to the United States in 1898. As a result, the population of Hawaiian language speakers dwindled, and with them, Hawaiian literature, for a time, ceased all together.

In the 1960s, Kanaka Maoli culture experienced a cultural and political renaissance, with a new generation of artists, musicians and writers emerging. Utilizing English, Hawaiʻi Creole English (popularly referred to as "Pidgin"), and ʻōlelo Hawaiʻi, early poets such as John Dominis Holt, Haunani-Kay Trask, Joe Puna Balaz, Puanani Burgess, Hoʻoipo DeCambra, Dana Naone Hall, ʻĪmaikalani Kalāhele, Wayne Kaumualiʻi Westlake and many others established a form of contemporary Hawaiian poetry which drew inspiration from both Hawaiian culture and outside influences.

Like the generations of Kanaka Maoli poets who have come before her, Sage Uʻilani Takehiro draws on traditional images of ʻāina and elements of nature—rain, wind, the ocean, cloud formations; moʻolelo—stories of our gods, ancestors, and heros; and moʻokūʻauhau—connection to family and community. Like the Kanaka poets documenting the Hawaiian experience with western colonialism from the nineteenth century to the present, in this collection of poems, Takehiro explores the intricacies of contemporary Kanaka cultural identity and effects of colonialism often resulting in various experiences of loss, anger, and violence. Yet despite the immeasurable suffering at the individual and collective levels, there is still hope, redemption, renewal found in the connection with ʻāina, heritage, tradition, honua.

An emerging voice of the next generation of Kanaka Maoli poets, Takehiro is as influenced by ʻōlelo Hawaiʻi, traditional images, and personal experience as much as by hip hop, reggae, and youth culture, intertwining the differing and sometimes competing influences into a solid, fresh perspective on contemporary Kanaka experiences on this honua, as part of this honua, today.

kuʻualoha hoʻomanawanui
Chief Editor, *ʻŌiwi: A Native Hawaiian Journal*

HONUA

Pō

Ke ahi i ka wai
oil pastel by Linus Chao

Pule Hoola

Aia Hilo a, ke ako mai a,
Ua paa mai a, kaupaku mai a,
Ke koli mai a, maikai mai a,
Poepoe mai a, papa ku mai a,
Papa ku mai la, ooki mai la,
O ka hale mai la, halii mai la ka mauu mai la,
Hohola mai la, ka moena mai la,
Uhia mai la ke kapa mai a,
Ka uluna mai a, ka moe mai — a,
Ke ala mai — la, ke ku mai la, ke hele mai la:
Hoolako mai — a, o ka ai mai a,
O ka ia mai — a, o ka wai mai — a; ke ai mai — a:
Ua pau mai — a, ka aina mai — a,
Holoi mai a, o ka lima mai — a;
Ke puka mai la, e.

A Prayer for Life

There Hilo is thatching,
Finishing, ridging,
Trimming until satisfactory,
Rounding off, boards standing.
Boards stood up and cut.
For the house there is spreading of the grass,
Unfolding and spreading of the mat,
Covering over with bed-clothes,
And using of pillows; there is sleeping,
Awaking, standing up and walking about.
There is preparation of food;
The fish and the water, there is eating.
There is the end to the eating,
There is washing of the hands,
And there is a coming out.

~Translation by Abraham Fornander~

"Me he makamaka lā nō ka ua o Hilo one"

The rain of Hilo bay is like a friend.

~Hālau o Kekuhi~

Self Medication

The people of Hilo are getting all rip.
The pipes whistle, they are high.
They drink alcohol until they feel good.
They take their shirts off and scrap each other in the earth.
They vomit. The stomach is reborn.
The mouth is rinsed; the gum is chewed;
The jacket is put on.
The designated drivers are drunk.
They rest their heads on the steering wheels; they sleep.
They awake, arise, and go forth.
They drive to Verna's,
Ken's, 7-11.
They eat.
They smoke cigarette.
They drop their friends off at a sweetheart's house.
They go home.

Kāhea Kahi

At the time of the hot rain

Wave your wings, call the wind
open the calabashes of your Kūpuna
call the winds by their names
call to the sky with your breath
when puhaiku suck air into your beak
You are an Owl…Fly!

If wings are weak, turn
your beak into gray fish gills
swim from sky into sea
call currents of Kanaloa
to carry you—water wind
winding through a world of Kai
You are a Shark…breathe ocean water through your skin

Don't be afraid of deep-sea darkness
Don't be afraid of light from the sky

Don't call on the rain this night

Kāhea I Ka Wā Pono

E Hui Pū

E Hui Pū!
E Hui Pū!

Aia i hea nā Kānaka?

Call them from their homes
wherever they may be

Call them from airports, hotels
call them from the sea

Call them from schools
restaurants, kitchens

Call them from parks,
beaches, benches

Call them from Kahiki,
continents, countries

Call them from farms,
loʻi, streams

Call them from buildings,
forests, jungles

Call them from jobs,
jails, gyms

Call all Kānaka,
dead or alive—flesh crawls
beneath skin

Call all Kānaka
smart and dumb—
if you don't get what this mele is saying
then don't ask me
ask your mana

Call all Kānaka
for better or for worse
death doesn't part us
mana never dies

Trace its movements with your tongue
taste its tracks, swallow its spirit
let it carry your eyes
Look at Us
E nānā iā Kākou, E 'ike i ka 'ī

Our bones hide from bulldozers
in the dirt breast of our mother
while the bones of our ancestors
breathe under our brown skins

born from the same darkness
As the Mo'o
We change colors

Mana Never Dies

Call the owl, the honu, the pig
ask for guidance, peace, and pua

Call the shark, the manō, the hunter
ask him to swim circles around us,
pull fish into our nets, and feed
knowledge into our piko, stir whispers
of star to ocean—whispers to the na'au

Calling all Kānaka

E hui pū
E hui pū Kākou
E hui pū ka Mana
E hui pū no Hawai'i nei
E hui pū no nā Kānaka
E hui pū Kākou
E hui pū
E hui pū ē

Kou Lei

I was a fetal spirit born in the ti leaf womb of our mother

You uncurled my body and saw severed stems of white ginger
                                        layered over each other
        'awapuhi ke'oke'o standing side by side
                        braided tightly in fine fibers, woven
                into rope by loving hands
                                        that dangled
                                                on each end

You pressed your nose against me
                                kissed my fragrance
                        and opened your eyes as you returned your breath

You held me in my ti leaf cradle, saw the brown footprints of rain
        and 'A'ala Honua that blows through the strands of your hair

                You knew that I slept on a bed of ginger roots
                                        drizzled with dirt

                You watched my petals unfold and twist
        eyes of white ginger
                        jumbled into my wrists as I rubbed them, crying
for Honua to feed my flowers
                        while forbidden blossoms were held firm
                by the rope bones of my body

                You peeled me from the ti-leaf and held me against your chest
I wrapped my arms around you and you tied my hands behind your
        neck
                                my mana
                        carried by yours

                I lay on top of your shoulders
                        listening to our life beat
                                through your skin
You carry my beauty
                while I breathe yours

                I am your lei

His Words Cut Me

My stomach hangs out
cut open and exposed

I hold the wound with the palms of my hands
my fingertips black with blood

Kanakas are stupid
Kanakas are lazy

My fingers dig into my flesh—
I'm not stupid. I'm not lazy.

Words bleed out of my stomach
I am too weak to fight back

Stupid Kanaka
He laughs to his own joke, his own serious joke
Stupid Kanaka

Daddy says the Kanakas don't know shit
don't know because they were forced to forget

Daddy thinks no one else feels the pain
of Mana, ignored

Daddy thinks he's alone
his best friends are the Trees, the Mud and the Rain
the Flowers are his sisters
the Birds are his lovers.

Daddy knows the Ocean, too.
They didn't get along at first
because the Ocean tried to eat Daddy
so ever since, he's been afraid
but I know the Ocean loves Daddy.

Daddy knows the spirit of the world
they talk, hang out and fight, just like family

Daddy knows the land is alive
Daddy knows this in his stomach

But his brain says
Kanakas are stupid
Kanakas are lazy
He thinks, he laughs, he fears—He knows

He's not stupid. He's not smart.
He is connected—to everything.

Daddy's voice
has mana.

It cuts through my stomach
and I hold bleeding words in the palms of my hands.

Fish Bones

Fish bones don't bother me.
It's dose damn multi-vitamins
dat get stuck right smack daddy in my esophagus

and das if
dey make it past my troat.
Sometimes, gotta buss 'um in half

but den da buss in half part
stay like sandpepa
scratching all against my grinding tube.

Anden, I get acid reflux
cuz da damn ting
stay stopping da gas flows

You know what I'm saying?
Den ho man, gotta chase 'um
down wit' choke wada—

J'like when you grine da fish bone
You like drink wada
But das not cuz da bone

stay stuck. Is cuz da fish
is so damn salty!
Da fish bones, just grine 'um.

Chase dat bugga wit' rice or poi
and you all good.
No need take multi-vitamin.

Ho Cuz

Chico Boy wen catch dirties from dat huge guy
Sean Sometin', Puna Boy,
at the raging Pōhaku pahday, when was

Friday I tink so. Anyways, da guy was all rip.
Chico Boy too—he wen pound one bottle 99 Bananas
before we even wen shoot 'um out to da pahday. Anden
him and Jonny wen shot gun da whole fricken case can Budlight
on da side a da road—Boom right dea da guy Sean

he came walking out da pahday all nuts
head butting all kine cahs, shcreaming,
"Who da fuck wen false my braddah, hah?
Who da fuck wen false my braddah?"

Den Chico Boy, all rip, he tell, "Oh,
dat ugly fucken kid dat was perving out on all da chicks?"
Ho, right dea, da Puna Boy wen rush Chico, boom!
False crack one time. Chico was wobbling.

Nex morning Chico call up Jonny on da phone
all hanging, "Jonny, brah, wea da fuck my tooth stay?"
Jonny wen tell 'um, "Eida stay on da side of the road out Pōhaku
or you wen eat dat fucka, cuz boi, you wen catch mean cracks.
I had fo' fucken pound tree guys cuz of you last night, you fucka."

Right dea, Jonny call me today buss laughing, "Brah,
Chico jus wen call me up fo' tell me
had only one, big, white corn in his shit. He was like
'Why I get corn in my shit, I neva eat corn.' So he wen look
moa close, was his fucken tooth!" I trip.

Suicidal Reflections

Eh, son. Whatchu tink,
Daddy should shoot himself o what?

I jus' figa, if yo' moddah no like be with me,
an evrybody stay telling me I one shitty foddah
cuz dey always gotta take kea my kid.

No sense I live—why, so I can burden everybody?
I always pissing everybody off anyways.

Babe always bitching at me
all I spend my money on is weed, and
she gotta pay fo' all her kid stuff. So
if I dead, das one less mout' she gotta
feed, ah? Mo' food fo' you.

                                                     Den she no need
bitch me out anymoa, no need fly stuff at me.
No need cry to her friends
I went give her lickens
cuz she always like go out pahtay.

Good, let my moddah guys take kea my son.
Dey take kea you mo' bettah den me—

I jus' bring you to da beach
drink bia, check out chicks,

an' da only stories I get fo' tell you
is about yoa crazy unkos scrapping guys
bare balls cuz dey no like dirty dea clothes
an' dey no ca affohd fo' buy bibadees—
plus too no sense wea bibs, das only fo' get
ball-rash wen u pau surf. Anyways,
You betta off not even knowing me.

So I figa, end dis bullshit already.
Den she going miss me,

                              and I going be like,
'Too late, bitch, you shoulda tought about dat
befo' I wen shoot myself.' But eh,

she can do whateva she like—Good!
Let her teach my son fo' be dakine perfeck,
sensitive, smaht guy I neva going be

cuz—oh shit! I going be dead! But fuck, boi
what I going do? I no can go sku,
dat place is mo' stupid den me! Shit.

Das why I neva like geeve yo' moddah monay
fo' sen you to presku
bumbye dey only going tell

you dumb. So what,
I should shoot myself?
You going tink I one asshole eeda way.

Look yo' moddah coming.
I gave her monay fo' fix dat damn
headlight, why she neva fix um yet?!
Stupid bitch, had fo' go do her nails as why.

Kay gimme kiss. No worry, I come visit you.
And Eh, I not going let you die like me
so no sense you try kill yo'self
cuz you only going make ass.

And nex time, tell yo' moddah
No Ack.

Noa

I ku mau mau...
I KU WA!

Chicken skin.

I ku mau mau, I ku huluhulu, I ka lanawao...
I KU WA!
I ku lanawao
I KU WA

Storm waves consume river eyes
salt splashes down sullen cliff faces

I KU WA HUKI
I KU WA KO
I KU WA A MAU
A MAU KA EULU...

He lifts his mother's chin
she looks to the ceiling of the funeral hall
closes her eyes.

E HUKI E
KULIA!

The Blue and Gold
football boys huddle
over an open casket
Alaka'i's cracked voice cries

I ku mau mau...

He swipes his cheek
with the back of his hand

I KU WA!
I ku mau mau, I ku huluhulu, I ka lanawao

Voices catch on fire.

I KU WA
I ku lanawao
I KU WA

The huddle stands straight
the voices grow strong
they open their breath to the heavens

I KU WA HUKI
I KU WA KO
I KU WA A MAU
A MAU KA EULU
E HUKI E…

Their voices pull him
out of the ground—

…KULIA!

Memories are born.

I ku mau mau…

Darkness. The lights of a town
flickered and died. Darkness.

I KU WA!

We were loud
drunk and high.
There were no lights
on that wide, dead end
lane in Pana'ewa

I ku mau mau…no homes
I ku huluhulu…no wings
I ka lanawao…no anchor

I KU WA!

We floated under the stars

I ku lanawao

Among the tall forest trees

I KU WA
I KU WA HUKI

Cops! Cops! Cops!

I KU WA KO

We threw our beer bottles in the bushes
and scattered like a scared school of fish

I KU WA A MAU

Where we going?
Four Miles! Four Miles!

Hurry up, jump in
Jump In!
Ho, Raging!
Lights brah, Lights.

A MAU KA EULU

Ooooh Shiiittt…

E HUKI E…

The Wal-Mart lights went out.
The telephone pole crashed into the car.

KULIA!

The lights are loud.
The people are silent.

He lifts his mother's chin
toward the ceiling of Dodo Mortuary,
flies over his open casket
and carries his Blue and Gold
teammates to survived family members
where his spirit stands free.

Noa.

Kahi

Mauna Kea
watercolor by Linus Chao

Fucken

Mālama the fucken ʻāina!
Mālama the fucken ʻāina!
Mālama the fucken ʻāina!

> The fucken ʻāina
> > Fucken ʻāina
> > > ʻāina
> > > ʻāina fucks
> > > > fuck
> > > > fuck the ʻāina
> > > > fuck the ʻāina

No need get married, just fuck

> Fuck the ʻāina.

Make babies
Make kalo
Make ulu
Make life

> Fuck the ʻāina

> *but make sure you get checked*
> *you don't wanna*
> *introduce no sicknesses*
> *to our land*
> *like feces to the ocean*
> *and coquis spreading like Chlamydia*
> *across the Big Island vagina*

> > *Make love to the ʻāina*

> > *Fuck her in the shower*
> > *and in the streets*
> > *Fuck her like she's the girl of your dreams*

> Fuck the ʻāina

Fuck her like she's your favorite side tap
the one you feel in your heart
but block out in your head.

Fuck the ʻāina

Fuck her like she's a best friend in need of your care.

Make love to the ʻāina
    Fuck the ʻāina
        ʻāina
        ʻāina fucks

She made babies with the rain
and had a love affair with a pig
A farmer threw some shit on her
but they had some beautiful kids

Fuck the ʻāina.
Make love to her

She calls us
to come and lay in her dirty bed

Make love to her
Fuck the ʻāina,
        ʻāina
        ʻĀina
        ʻĀina makes love

      Fucken ʻāina love
              Love fucken ʻāina
              Love fucken
        Fucken love
           Love
                  Love makes love
                    Makes love
                    Makes

```
              Make
              Make love
                    Love
                    Love Fuck
                          Fuck
                          Fucken
                          Fucken love
              Make      Fucken love
              Make      Fucken love
```

Getting Warmer

```
Make Fucken Love
              Love to da 'Āina
                    To da 'Āina
                          'Āina
Make Fucken Love to da 'Āina!
Make Fucken Love to da 'Āina!
    Getting Hotter        'Āina
                          'Āina Fucks
                                Fucken 'Āina
                                Fucken 'Āina
                          the Fucken 'Āina
                                      'Āina
                                      'Āina
                                      'Āina mālama
                                            Mālama
                                            mālama 'Āina
                                                  'Āina
                                                  'Āina
                                            Mālama 'Āina
```

Mālama da fucken 'Āina!
Mālama da fucken 'Āina!

BURN

Sexual Frustration

I haven't got ass in a long time
at least one month already
my skin is getting white, so
I tell fuck this, fly my book on top
the ground and make 'um to da ocean
I Austin Powers it into one illegal stall
like a glove, jump out and rush 'um
run into the water, not Bay Watch style
but like a manini flopping on hot land
trying to work my way to Kanaloa

he makes me wet. I swim in salty waters
of love, warm and thick, dripping
down my throat, beading off my breasts
he carries me in the ocean bed, I float on
the tip of his head—it's firm and soft
sweet salty splashes of his sweat surround
me. His sea is filled with choke fish
I'm just one of them, but that's aight
with me cuz he always hits my G-spot

The tongues of Tangaroa tickle, while I
wriggle inside of him. Kāne, slowly penetrates—
blows sweet smoke, sprays it in the space
between him and me. I breathe deep
sucking him into me

                                Mmmmm…I stay
moaning and all kay, and the only other one
who can hear is Kanaloa; he holds me
as I breathe kisses from Kāne. He licks
my wet skin while I sway my hips for him
I breathe like life is breathing through me
I breathe until my body is satisfied.
Sometimes it comes super fast
sometimes it comes super slow
but the frustration always comes out
no matter what, as long as I'm
fucking the Sky.

Hina

I am in love with her
the fragrance of moonflower
wakes me from my sleep

I peek through a screen
to watch her undress
she sways her moonlight hips
slides soft across my face

I drink her breath
hungry for her mind
thirsty for her life

I suck her soft
swollen lips that drip
into the harvest nights

I crave her
she is the rhythm of kapa
pounding through roots in my heart

I make love to her beauty
swallow her light
it swims through my stomach
and bleeds out of my maʻi

I am in love with her
Hina

God is Pregnant

His womb swells, tears
rip open his ravished vagina
birthplace of kalo and us

dark and wet he breathes
rising with the rain and the tides
he sighs, "poor keiki...

bumbye they learn."
Kānaka cruise to da promised land
paddles up, pull, pulling

pulled by the star flames
of our father. The exodus of the outcast
move to the waʻa rhythm

of our hearts. Spirits skank
across the sky, our feet are tired
and bleeding. Flesh cries

dancing to the beat that booms
through our veins. His waterfalls
fertilize his rivers and flow

from between his hairy legs
drips into his womb, swollen
and torn. Kalo born from his dark

breath, heaved through
the promised land by hands
of his sun. We wriggle

out of his wet womb, swollen
and stink, it pushes us toward
the promised place

star flame tugs umbilical cords, burns
the scabs of our minds. Blood drips
through a piko, pulled by the promised

'āina—raped, ravished
and spit on by one-eyed monster
dick heads.

God lays screaming, legs
strapped to a maternity bed

                                        He gives birth to kalo and us

Lā

Hāmākua After Rain
watercolor by Linus Chao

Vacation on Hawai'i's Big Island

You're coming to paradise,
but don't imagine grass huts on the beach—
extremely modern and sophisticated
Tents and Tarps only.

Complete professionals treat you with aloha.
Renew, refresh, amaze and deeply touch
spectacular unspoiled nature—
Government Housing Restrictions Do Not Apply.

Uniquely nourish the warmth of authentic aloha spirit.
Feel the presence of this special place
natural wonders abound—
Please Do Not Feed the Animals.

Mysteries of outer space
touch the heavens
atop Mauna Kea—
Observatories are Closed Due to Massive Snowing.

Immerse yourself
in an ocean of total clarity, graceful beauty,
elusive grandeur and spectacular scenic vistas.
Blaze the afternoon away.

Fire demonstrates power.
Fiery scenes fast flowing underground,
slow tempo of surface flows
Descend into the sea.

Next on Wild On E!
Playboy's newest issue features
Fire Goddesses at Hawai'i's
Steamy Volcano!

Eager visitors flock
dominate the landscape
fierce glow of red heat crawls
Spectacular Kīlauea Show.

Fertile lava landscapes of
lush greenery, cool and misty ʻōhiʻa
Spring forth and flourish—

17-year-old Keahi Hoʻoulu is pregnant
with her second child; she dropped
out of high school to clean toilets at

The Breathtaking, Fantastic
Hawaiʻi Volcanoes National Park
Open 24 hours every day of the year!

Forests
of verdant plantlife
dance legendary hula in the
Rain.

Savor succulent exotic hues
of a colorful culture mix that
pampers, restores and heals
Your Body and Your Spirit.

Hawaiʻi's whole culture
is based on Aloha—
and that's a commitment we take
Very Seriously.

Progress at Pōhakuloa

You go explode your spear in Iraq, Hawaiian Warrior, and I will cast my pen and fling stones with my tongue—either way, we move forward. Without you I stand alone in this beautiful part of Pōhakuloa, giving a braided ti-leaf lei in lamentation for the dirt under this American Military Training Camp.

Love this dirt with me Hawaiian Warrior, as you do every day of your career, guarding the entrance to the American Military Training Camp. Love this dirt that gave birth to your Grandfather, whose Maui tongue gives you chicken skin. Let our flesh crawl together. I will cry for Pōhakuloa and give her tears to you, while you stand strong. Both our feet firmly planted in Papahānaumoku.

E Hawaiian Warrior, I not pau yet. Your thick brown lips say, "No can survive if we go back to da ancient days." If I were to pluck out your 'Ōiwi eyes they would bleed, pulsate and die. Plopped on this dirt, your dried eyeball juice will ejaculate in your wahine and those 'Ōiwi eyes will generate in your children. They will come and give love to this dirt that they come from. How do you wish them to see it?

Everybody makes like the American Military is so bomb, so solid, so nuts. What about the ground that they train on? What about Papahānaumoku? You wonder why they get mana—cuz they tax it from Hawai'i!

But you are generous; you give your mana to them, eager to fight the battle in your blood. "I am proud to be Hawaiian," you say. Say it again. Say it everyday. Say it out loud so she can hear you. Papahānaumoku brought me to Pōhakuloa to trespass against the illegitimate Federal Property that you guard firmly. She brought me here to cry to you so that you would say, "I am proud to be Hawaiian."

She watches you work long hours everyday at Pōhakuloa. She sees the way you look at her, like you are in love. She wants you to say it out loud so everyone can hear you say, "I am proud to be Hawaiian." She is not ancient. She stands before you. She will stand after you. She stands in beauty, despite the unexploded ordnances scattered like pimples on her nose.

She loves us, as we are her children. Care for her so that she can care for you. Love her. Love her out loud. Aloha. She forgives you Hawaiian Warrior. She forgives me. Let us give our breaths to her together. She is our Earth Mother.

(By the way Americans, try dropping one "Thanks Ah" at least to the 'Āina for holding your military's fierce feet that supposedly can kick the world's ass.)

Dis Poem

Dis poem is not permanent
das why I write um in pencil

cuz he going fade
to da oddah side a da page

drip tru da book covah
an leave come stains on da bed.

Dis journal, dis pepa, dis napkin
hard an trobbing, thic wit words,

some 'ono, I tell you.
Wooo, broke da mouth

broke da eye, broke da ear
broke da stereo.

Sound spits
from da napkin, da receipt, da hand,

grab 'um wit da teet
da tongue; all blood.
suck 'um out-push 'um
down da troat, swallow 'um.

Wake up, take one shit.
Going have little pieces a dis poem,
da pahts da stomach
no could handle, smashed inside.

But da res, da rest a dis poem
stay in da love handles, da ass, da tighs,
da gut. Den going burn

in da gym, yoga class, hula,
on da ocean or on da lunch break
when wala'auing

because I tol' you,
dis poem ain't permanent

Kumulipo Remix

Born is everything from the dark
and the slime, where another world

swirls words to life with a tongue
lungs suck the breath of an ocean

beyond paʻa concrete civilization
realization and rediscovery reveals captivity

of mana carved in the naʻau
now, born from a petroglyph
poem is her kino

she hears the song of the ʻIʻiwi
singing to the ʻŌʻō, who are off
somewhere breeding

bleeding their feather plucked pubes
in a forest where the pig digs into the earth

birth is the uprooted tracks of Kamapuaʻa
pimpin' nā pua and making moʻo women
wet in the night

Born are his domestics with Pele
who wen pound Hiʻiaka
for fooling around with Lohiʻau

they made out on the staircase
spread legs and did it doggy style

while the ʻŌʻō nested on the roof, in the kaʻa
and on the ʻAʻā at Makuʻu where
pūpū are pounded by the sways of Kanaloa's maʻi
against the pali of Papahānaumoku

Born are the songs of sex
sucking mana through
slime that breathes life

Born are the kamaliʻi o kēia mau moʻolelo
Here we are, the children of Hawaiʻi
eia mākou, nā mele hoʻokani
here we are, the leaders of tomorrow
oli ē, oli ē no mākou
Born are the passions from the kūpuna
Born are the dances to the people
Born are the stories for the keiki

Born is the blood of Kānaka
and the spirit of Kumulipo through
the wormhole womb of Pō

Born are the prisons of our world
and the oli we conceive in them
they cage a voice singing poems
to the ʻŌʻō birds, who are off somewhere
breeding

'Anakala Kalāhele's Love-Hate Lecture

In dis worl', only can Love or Hate. Cuz all get in between is frustration and jealousy. And dat, no can. Sometimes you trip out, you trip out, you trip out some moa—nex ting you know you tripping all ova da place until sometin pull on da Love line—Boom, you fall down, den pau. Stan up feeling like one champ all smiles and Nobody, not No-damn-fricken-body, can tax your mana because you—Because You—get da powa, fo' geeeve 'um! Keep 'um, eat 'um, do what feel good to you man, do whatevah feel goood to you.

Sometimes, some individuals, dey gotta Hate. Dey no can help. Like when da wahine get dea da kine, dea ma'i ah, Hooo—Watch Out! Dea homones li'dat stay getting all nuts. Dey trip out, dey trip out, dey trip out some moa cuz dey gotta go work, dey gotta do dis, dey gotta do dat. But for real kine brah all dey like do is lay down an eat chocolate Hagendaz. Nah, no need be Hagendaz but gotta be chocolate brah. Gotta be chocolate, cuz chocolate tastes like looove. An when da wahine stay trippin', gotta geeve 'um Love—Even if she ready fo' buss yo' eye cuz you tol' her neva have chocolate…"But no worry, no worry Bebe, get Rocky Ro-oad"…Ok, she pau be piss off, grab da spoon, scoop da mashmello, melt 'um on her toungue. Den oooh, she Looove you—until she bite into one nut, den ho man she get all nuts…"My teet soah, my back soah, my whole body soah— You No Undastan!"…"No Bebe, I dunno whatchu talkin' about. But I Looove you!"

Sometimes, some people, dey jus hate cuzzz—Ahh Dunno? Dey get problems as why. But everybody get problems and da ting not going kill you—If you Love 'um. But if you hate 'um den sorry brah, you dead. But if you Love death den death going Love you back but you not going be dead. And if you hate death then death going hate you back and you going be dead brah, you going be dead, pau, no can. Hate is stale. Hate is stink. Hate is souah. Hate is Uuugly, brah, Hate is fucken Uuugly. Hate is hamajang.

In dis worl', everybody Love. Sometimes individuals trip out, dey get frustrated, dey get jealous a da people who no feel hamajang like dem—Anden, Boom!—Sometimes, in dis worl', everybody Hate. But imagine one stale worl' all stink, all souah, all fucken Uuugly—no can. Da pilikia going come brah, da pilikia going come, trip you out, trip you out, try tax your mana, try kill you. But you get da powa Braddah, Sista, Cuz, you get da powa fo' breathe, fo' keep da 'ea circulating so no come stale, no come stink, no come souah. So mo' bettah Love den Hate brah, mo bettah love den hate—you know why? Cuz can.

What Stoners Think About When They're Getting Stoned

I was going buy one 20
but even da Mountain View guys stay selling um by da eights
nobody get small bags anymoa
das da kine, economic inflation
due to too much legal risks in da mahket.
Stupid ass war on drugs.
Why dey no boddah da crackheads, or da pill freaks
C'mon Uncle Harry
rehabilitation if anyting
cuz eradication only going piss people off.

So anyways, I wen drive all da way Mountain View
buy one eight ounce shetty weed and one goat
all fo' hunred bucks. Not bad.

My granmaddah, 79 yeas ol'
and she's still weed whacking da yahd
I tol' her she bettah go easy
wit' her high blood presha
but she no like listen.
She complain Tūtū Man no help her do nottin'
around da house, cuz she get brown skin.
She tell if she had white skin he would listen
but he Japanee—tink he too good fo' do house work
she tell, yeah Japanee fo' nothin'
he no mo monay.

Pua Tūtū Man.
He no can do da kine heavy yahd work any moa
cuz he get prostate problems
he going shit his pants!
Sometimes he no can even make 'um to da batroom
den Tūtū Lady make him scrub da rug,
Pua ting.

So I wen spen half my paycheck on dat damn goat
put 'um in da yahd
only fo' Tūtū Lady scream at me,

"Who going clean up the goat shit?!"
But eh, at leas' dey no need cut grass.

I bought da weed fo' me an Marie.
Marie's las' name use to be 'Īmaikalani
but she got married aftah graduation
anden she wen change 'um to Wise.
Me and Marie get stoned at Four Miles Wall evry day.
Marie cannot not be stoned.
She gotta tune out da world,

tune out da law,
tune out time,
tune out da monay she no moa,
tune out da genitals she was grabbing da night befoa
tune out da oddah braddah dat she was trying fo' tune out da
    oddah day
tune out da guys dat tink dey da shit—
big for nothin' faggots, gotta false girls
fohce herself fo' smoke some moa
training fo' scrap her husband when she go home
'cuz she was stoning out at da wall wit' me

Fohget it. Fohget tuning out da world
fohget getting fucked up
fohget getting married
fohget graduating high sku
fohget what we neva learn in high sku
Fohget da tings we do fo' fohget

Stoners fohget evryting.
I fohgot fo' feed my granmaddah's goat
den I wen remembah dat I fohgot dat da goat going eat da grass—
Oh, so das why da ting was outside
cruising in da pouring rain.
I was going put 'um in da dog kennoh
but den Tūtū Man wen whack my head

wit da mango pickah—Ho, watch out Tūtū Man,
no shit your pants!
Nah fertalizah.

He tell, "Eh you stupid! Jus' geeve 'um wada
go put 'um in da grass!
You like da dogs eat goat fo' dinnah
hah Yuki, you like eat goat tonight?!
Hah, hah, heh, heh, hegh, cough, cough…"

Cough, cough, cuuuaaaah…
Ho brrraah, dis weed is harsh, I stay tearing an all
huh-uuh…Eh try make one crutch Marie
right dea can use my boss' business cahd—Eh fuck you!

You wish you had one job at Wal-Mart
Bitch, nex time buy yoa own damn weed—
Eh, iz not my fault you married to one broke ass haole
half rich, half pua, no can pay rent, no can qualify fo' couny housing.
Shit, mo bettah marry one half Hawaiian
at leas' dey put chu on da waiting lis'!

A Letter

To the Executive Council of the Provisional Government of Hawai'i, Mr. Sanford B. Dole, President; Mr. James A. King, Minister of the Interior; Mr. William O. Smith, Attorney General; and Mr. Peter C. Jones, Minister of Finance:

WHATCHU FUCKAS!!!

I like twis' my fingas in yoa skanky ass beards
pull yoa faces down hard
against my knee, buss all yoa fucken teeth. Mutha Fuckas.

I like spit fire atchu wit dis boiling breath
burn off all da skin
on da back of yoa neck. Mutha Fuckas.

But da 'Aumākua stay telling me, "Shut the fuck up.
Look da Queen cruising in her pimp ride carried in between yellow
    and red Kāhili
Wit Kānaka on the rise." But Fuck,

I HATE YOU. Mutha Fuckas.

I like dig my hand inside yoa eye balls
puncture da pupils wit my nails
Broke yoa sinus bone wit' my middle fingah grip and rip 'um out yoa
    fucken stuck-ass nose. Mutha Fuckas.

But no can. Not cuz you dead already
and not cuz I scayed scrap yoa great, great grandkids
But cuz da 'Aumākua stay telling me, "Shut the fuck up, Mutha
    Fucka."

So I going listen to da 'Aumākua, and I going shut da fuck up. I ain't
    giving you my voice no moa.

(Fucken Donkeys.)

Moe

Chanting
watercolor on silk by Jane Chao

Operation Liberation: Let Kanaloa Breathe

We're breaking down the break
wall, darkness returns to the depths
of the sea—Let's catch waves in our canoes, hoe

wa'a like race cars on kai, cut
commercial fishing lines, bust
boulders and smash stones with our heart

beat blades that circulate Kanaloa's blood, dig
into his flesh, ripped and smiling
under the sun like guns in paddlers' arms. Pa'akai

drips down pāpa'a skin—We're gonna win!
Sea bound journeys stretched across the Pacific
discoursed to races representing Polynesia

and then some—they come from all kine places
parts of Papa that you've never seen
with polluted eyes swimming blind

at the bottom of Hilo Bay. Breached
in a boat harbor belly, Kanaloa's broken tongue calls out
to waters stagnant behind stones. His throat open

ready to swallow, we chew until we choke
with shark teeth blades biting the Break Wall
one nibble at a time, we're gonna let Kanaloa breathe

Ka Uʻi o nā Waʻa Mālia

Hoʻopuka nā puna i kai o Hilo One
Me nā waʻa mālia e holoholomoku
Ua puka nā waʻa mai nā puna a Hilo One
ʻO ka lani e honi nei i Mauna Kea
Aia o Poliʻahu i ka wao akua
Ke akua mai nei, ke akua mai
Hoʻopōmaikaʻi me ka ua kea
Kaʻalele aʻela nā waʻa, me ka puna i ke kai
Kaʻalele aʻela ka mana a wāhine
Kaʻalele mua ka waʻa mālia
Ka waʻa mālia o puna Hilo One
O Hilo One ē, O Hilo One ē
ʻO Hilo One e pūlama nei
Pūlama i nā waʻa mālia
A lamalama nā waʻa mālia
E lamamlama ē, e lamalama ē
E lamalama nā waʻa mālia
He mele no nā puna o Hilo One.

ʻAuhea ka uʻi o nā waʻa mālia, e Uʻi

E Uʻi, your look is lookin'
so sweet—Everytime you swing that smile
back at me, beneath the mountain
kissing sky so heavenly
I feel like flying, with one eye winkin'
at the sea. Hey Uʻi, hope when my flying

wish comes true, I'll be riding low
in a mālia canoe, cruising with your crew
wanna sail past the paʻa rock wall, wanna
surf the swells and all
always stopping by the green bouy
Hey Uʻi, I'll be waiting for you

Kamani tree is where I'll be, burying blades
from a mālia canoe—Can't wait 'till you
come back inside with me, where waves rising

hypnotize and strokes surprise
the other guys, who going cry
'cause we went fly right by them

Hey Uʻi, please stay with me
under the moon, please don't say
you'll be leaving soon, please swing that smile
back at me. Kamani tree is where I'll be
waiting for you, waiting in
a mālia canoe

Haʻina ʻia mai ana ka puana lā
ʻAuhea ka uʻi o nā waʻa mālia
ʻAuhea ka uʻi o nā waʻa mālia

Ka Wailani O Hilo

go to sleep now
words crawl through your eyes
education invades your mind
rest your head upon the pages
of decolonization
and recolonization
and government operation
kill, steal, deceive
Dream
maile around your neck
you're going to a place
where a stone wall breaks
waves, as they cruise into a black bay
feel the wind hug you
and squeeze your shoulders
the warm sun flares a sky
of 'onolicious colors
that brown your skin, while
ice rushes through the veins of Wainaku
melts into the sobering ponds
of an ocean where pua melia are
hung over
from bolts of rain that shoot
from revolving clouds
like liquid bullets, they crack the asphalt
Roots of dead Koa
drink water from the Sky Father
Roots of dead warriors live again
and paradise cries
our paradise cries
Uē, paradise lies
rest now
don't wake up
don't leave your dreams
stay with the wild Hau trees
that shade the shores of Keaukaha
dance with the Liko Lehua
that rain below the mountains

draped in Snow
sing with the Palapalai
that echo through the caves of Kaumana
blow with the Puakenikeni
in the gold winds of Pana'ewa
stay with the water
just beyond the gracious green Grass
where the honu surfs
broken waves, where Manini
swim around your legs
Know more things in your dreams
than you could possibly see
with your eyes open to all
the words of the world
know the ocean cooled by snow
know the cries of clouds
and the morning tears of flowers
Dream
Dream of the rain
Dream of home
go to sleep now
go to the water of the heavens

Kāhea Hou

At the time when the Mountains are on fire
At the time when the birds fly away from thick smoke
At the time when snails hide themselves in the cool earth

Don't call on the wind
  this night.

Call on the currents of Kanaloa
  to carry the rains
    from Hawai'i to Kaua'i

Call on the manō
  to swim circles around Oahu
    pull rain in to Nānākuli

Call on the rain clouds
  of Haleakalā
    Nā Ulu, Nā Ulu, Nā Ulu
    come and block the winds from Nānākuli

Call on the Hilo rain
  to pour on Nānākuli

Call on the Wailua rain
  to pour on Nānākuli.

Don't call on the wind this night.

Kāhea i ka wā pono.

Ha'ina 'ia mai ana ka puana

Me he makamaka lā nō ka ua o Hilo one

~Hālau o Kekuhi~

Honua

1. Land

The solid ground of the earth
in a distinct area or region
Born from liquid fire
Born from black rocks
that give birth to sand
at the sea.

2. Earth

The productive soil surface
of the world
Brown as mud after rain
Brown as skin after sun
Black as the flesh
of the third victim of the sun
Black as the hair spiked
against the pigs back
who uproots the fertility of Hiʻiaka.

3. World

The realm or domain
of a particular way of life
where mortals exist
and spirits rise from red eyes
that squint and say A Hui Hou

to the sun as it melts into another world
while feet slip through the milky sand
of Hāpuna and waves come forth,
consuming footprints, and digests them
into the belly of the sea.

4. Background

The area or surface against
which Sugar Cane is seen
on the coast of Hāmākua

against the roofs of homes
and the white lines of broken
waves in blue water
and the white lines of
scudding clouds in the blue Sky.

One's total experience
of Eurocentric Education
and knowledge obtained
by listening to the savage ocean
and by reading the illiterate
vocabulary of the sky.
I memorized the chemical composition
of clouds, but I know when the rain comes
because I smell cloudy emotions
as faces turn from white
to Gray.

I learned the music of the Wind
and the voices of trees
that are uncivilized and untamed.

5. Foundation

The basis of underlying support.
My grandfather gave me the stars
  to see in the dark.
My grandfather gave me a painting
  of Green Bamboo.
My grandmother gave me a valley
  called Waipi'o.
My grandmother gave me a painting
  of heavenly beauty.
My mother taught me
  to dance in the rain.
My father taught me
  to eat the bones of dried fish.

My sisters taught me
  to write by pissing me off
  and being too big for me to beat up
So my pen cried on the pages of a pink diary.

Endowed institutions taught me lies.
  Christopher didn't discover America.
  James didn't discover Hawai'i.
  Trigonometry will not help me in the grocery store
  and the SATs are rigged.

Intermediate time I learned how to roll a joint.
  Mrs. Himphill gave me a form for my mother to sign
  that would allow me to advance to AP Social Studies.
  After school, I shredded the form and fed it to the fish
  in a river where I swam with friends and smoked joints.
High School is where I went on Fridays
to find out where the parties were.
I also had perfect attendance
at Saturday School.

6. Environment

The circumstances that surround one.
Time pulled the sun out from the horizon
with the cords of my voice.

I watched the radiant energy
peak through a cloudy window
where pink angels danced between the earth and sky.

Then the dawn smelled ginger
and the ti-leaves shook the rain
off from its limbs.

I walked down the black sand
to the corner of an old building

where English was a foreign language
and anthuriums bathed in dirty white buckets.

I pulled a dollar out of my bra
and put it on a wrinkled hand
of crooked fingers and dirty nails.

Then I ate my poi mochi
under a Banyan near a cliff of
broken glass from beer bottles
that screamed memories of dancing in the rain.

Ka Ua Wahi Lani

'Auhea wale ana 'oe i ka ua lā
me ke ana noe i ka ua wahi lani

Kūlewa ke ka'oka'o o Wai'ale'ale lā
'O ka Noelehua e kālewa nei

Kiawe mai ke kapakapa a ka He'enehu
Kālunu ke ka'apeha a hao mai nei lā

Ku papu Hilo i ka ua wehiwa lā
Kau ko Hilo wai lani i Wao Akua

'O Lilinoe ke hahau nei i Wailuku lā
Ha'aloku ka makakēhau a Wainaku

Hō'eu a'ela Kamakaniniho'ole
Na ke Kinimaka Lehua i pā hili

Hekili ho'i ka ua Pupūhale lā
E ho'āo nei ke aokū me ka ua hō'e'elo

Hawewe 'o Kuāua me ka 'elo'elo
Hākuma 'o Wa'awa'ahia a'o Waipi'o

Kilika'a, Kilihune, Kilinahe, mai kiohoa
Pūloku ke aka'ula, mai hilahila

Kīkaha ke kiawe'ula me ke kilikili
Kawewe 'o Ililani iā Nāulu o Kawaihae

Kapakē ka wela o ka ua ma ke kai
Pūnohu ka uahi wai i loko o Ka'au lā

'O Kohala i ka wao ma'ukele lā
Aia ka ua pūnohu 'ohu'ohu

Kīpū ke Kīpu'upu'u, mai pōhe'eua
E mā'au lāua i ka loku o ka mākuma

Ua ū ʻo Waimea i ka pulupuluʻelo
E liko nei ka liko a ka Waiʻapo

Ulupē nā manu i ka ua Kinailehua lā
Ua hili i ke kīhene lehua panopaʻū

Pū me ka hili maiʻa hoʻi ke aloha la
ʻO Kona Lani ke aloha mau loa

ʻUme ʻia ke Koʻiawe i ke Kualau,
ka ua nū hele ma ka moana i Kalae

Ua ʻapoa ke Koʻiawe i ka leo o Kaʻupena
Halihali ʻo ia iā Moaniani Lehua

Ka ua i wili ʻia me ka Līhau o Pāhoa
Nā ua hōʻīnana i ka huawaimaka

Leihiwa ʻo Punaʻala i ka wai ua
me ka haku wai lani kau mai i luna

Haʻina ʻia mai ana ka puana lā
me ke ana noe i ka ua wahi lani.

Pule Hoola Aia Hilo a, ke ako mai a, Ua paa mai a, kaupaku mai a, Ke koli mai a, maikai mai a, Poepoe mai a, papa ku mai a, Papa ku mai la, ooki mai la, O ka hale mai la, halii mai la ka mauu mai la, Hohola mai la, ka moena mai la, Uhia mai la ke kapa mai a, Ka uluna mai a, ka moe mai — a, Ke ala mai — la, ke ku mai la, ke hele mai la: Hoolako mai — a, o ka ai mai a, O ka ia mai — a, o ka wai mai — a; ke ai mai — a: Ua pau mai — a, ka aina mai — a, Holoi mai a, o ka lima mai — a; Ke puka mai la, e. Pule Hoola Aia Hilo a, ke ako mai a, Ua paa mai a, kaupaku mai a, Ke koli mai a, maikai mai a, Poepoe mai a, papa ku mai a, Papa ku mai la, ooki mai la, O ka hale mai la, halii mai la ka mauu mai la, Hohola mai la, ka moena mai la, Uhia mai la ke kapa mai a, Ka uluna mai a, ka moe mai — a, Ke ala mai — la, ke ku mai la, ke hele mai la: Hoolako mai — a, o ka ai mai a, O ka ia mai — a, o ka wai mai — a; ke ai mai — a: Ua pau mai — a, ka aina mai — a, Holoi mai a, o ka lima mai — a; Ke puka mai la, e. Pule Hoola Aia Hilo a, ke ako mai a, Ua paa mai a, kaupaku mai a, Ke koli mai a, maikai mai a, Poepoe mai a, papa ku mai a, Papa ku mai la, ooki mai la, O ka hale mai la, halii mai la ka mauu mai la, Hohola mai la, ka moena mai la, Uhia mai la ke kapa mai a, Ka uluna mai a, ka moe mai — a, Ke ala mai — la, ke ku mai la, ke hele mai la: Hoolako mai — a, o ka ai mai a, O ka ia mai — a, o ka wai mai — a; ke ai mai — a: Ua pau mai — a, ka aina mai — a, Holoi mai a, o ka lima mai — a; Ke puka mai la, e. Pule Hoola Aia Hilo a, ke ako mai a, Ua paa mai a, kaupaku mai a, Ke koli mai a, maikai mai a, Poepoe mai a, papa ku mai a, Papa ku mai la, ooki mai la, O ka hale mai la, halii mai la ka mauu mai la, Hohola mai la, ka moena mai la, Uhia mai la ke kapa mai a, Ka uluna mai a, ka moe mai — a, Ke ala mai — la, ke ku mai la, ke hele mai la: Hoolako mai — a, o ka ai mai a, O ka ia mai — a, o ka wai mai — a; ke ai mai — a: Ua pau mai — a, ka aina mai — a, Holoi mai a, o ka lima mai — a; Ke puka mai la, e. Pule Hoola Aia Hilo a, ke ako mai a, Ua paa mai a, kaupaku mai a, Ke koli mai a, maikai mai a, Poepoe mai a, papa ku mai a, Papa ku mai la, ooki mai la, O ka hale mai la, halii mai la ka mauu mai la, Hohola mai la, ka moena mai la, Uhia mai la ke kapa mai a, Ka uluna mai a, ka moe mai — a, Ke ala mai — la, ke ku mai la, ke hele mai la: Hoolako mai — a, o ka ai mai a, O ka ia mai — a, o ka wai mai — a; ke ai mai — a: Ua pau mai — a, ka aina mai — a, Holoi mai a, o ka lima mai — a; Ke puka mai la, e.

He lei no Hawai'i Nei

About the Author

The author (far right) with sisters Ruby Grace (left) and Jade Takehiro (middle).

Sage Uʻilani Takehiro, known as "Sager the Rager" to her friends, was born to Grace Chao and Paul Takehiro in Hilo, Hawaiʻi. Takehiro won her first writing award from Hilo Union School when she was in the first grade, graduated from Hilo High School in 2000, and graduated with high honors from the University of Hawaiʻi at Mānoa, with a BA in English and a BA in Political Science, where she has won the Myrle Clark and Ernest Hemingway Awards in creative writing. In 2006 she enrolled in UH–Mānoa's Master's Program in English. Takehiro is a political activist, community supporter, and a lover of the natural environment. Her work has been published in *TROUT, Tinfish, ʻŌiwi: A Native Hawaiian Journal,* and she writes the Pidgin column in the *Big Island Weekly. Honua* is her first book publication.

www.ingramcontent.com/pod-product-compliance
Lightning Source LLC
Chambersburg PA
CBHW021910040426
42447CB00007B/786